## Dedication

This book is dedicated to

Mervyn William Earle Carter (1895 – 1992)

in celebration of a life well lived

and to his enduring friendship with my father,

Rupert "Bert" Brooke Gratte (1896 – 1976).

## Acknowledgments

I am grateful to the following people and organisations who have all assisted with the writing of this book:

- ❖ Merve Carter's Grandsons Tim Collins, Frank Collins and Peter Collins who have taken this book from the original handwritten copy to its final digital format.

- ❖ The Shire of Kondinin.

- ❖ Tony Herring and Colin Nichols for information on the Wheatbelt Farms Scheme of the early days.

- ❖ Brent Hyde of Mt. Stewart Farms, the present-day owners of Merve Carter's block.

© 2025 Published by Tim Collins (tscollins7@gmail.com)

## Table of Contents

Preface ............................................................................ 7

The story of Mervyn William Earle Carter, 16$^{th}$ and 48$^{th}$ Battalions 9

Family ............................................................................. 9

Early Years ..................................................................... 10

The Great War ................................................................ 18

Merve's Wartime Story ................................................... 37

Merve's Life After The War ............................................. 40

Merve - Family and Farming ........................................... 45

Losing the Farm .............................................................. 50

Life in Wongan Hills ........................................................ 59

Appendix ........................................................................ 61

    Appendix 1 – Merve's handwritten memoir. ........................... 62

    Appendix 2 – Merve's statement to the AIF upon his return to Australia and the AIF's finding. ................................................ 99

    Appendix 3 – Newspaper articles covering Merve's bicycle road-racing exploits. .............................................................. 103

    Appendix 4 – Merve's letter to Bert Gratte. .......................... 104

## Preface

I grew up with a catskin rug on my bed in the wintertime. It contained many catskins of all colours, beautifully soft tanned, with an art-felt backing that had a border, artfully "pinkered."

My parents had a similar kangaroo skin rug on their bed, and our house had tanned fox and possum skins for chair covers. My father frequently went on hunting trips with his dogs, returning with beautiful pelts that he would then tan. He and Mum had made them into useful items with the aid of a sewing machine, which stood on our back veranda. He had learned to do all this from his boyhood friend, Merve Carter. It was really the trade of a "currier" rather than a "tanner," but they did tan leather, always using red gum from the red gum trees, which grew prolifically in the Northam district.

In the early 1920s, Dad and Merve got a small tannery going "at a spring out behind Northam High School." Dad was a clerical officer in the Northam Railways, and Merve was a labourer, so the tannery was a sideline. I know they advertised in the newspapers as I found one of their advertisements.

I guess Dad was more commercial, while Merve was more interested in making things from the leather and furs they produced. For reasons unknown, the tanning business was dissolved, and they parted company with Dad finishing up with most of the equipment, which makes me think that he had originally financed the venture. We still had all the equipment in 1935 when we moved to Geraldton, and Dad completed some orders he had when we arrived.

Merve continued tanning and making many artistic things with the produce. This included marvellously plaited stock whips, bridles, dolls, and harness repairs as a sideline. He also kept in touch with my relatives at the old Gratte family home, my Aunt Winn and Uncles Eric and Percy.

It seems I had always known the family legend of Merve's extraordinary exploits in World War I, which he had written up, though the manuscript had become lost. The manuscript, titled, **My Career Since 1914**, was later rediscovered and has become the inspiration for this book.


Stan Gratte OAM

# The story of Mervyn William Earle Carter, 16th and 48th Battalions

Mervyn William Earle Carter was born on April 30, 1895, in Northam, Western Australia, to William Forward Carter and Mary Eleanor Carter (née York). He was the fifth of eight children, growing up alongside his siblings, Vernon, Mena, Clarice, Ella, Bertrude (Bert), Rose, and Francis (Frank).

## Family

Merve's life was marked by both joyful and tragic events. He experienced early tragedy with the heartbreaking passing of his mother from measles when he was just seven years old in September 1902.

Following his mother's death, his father was unable to work and care for the children, resulting in the family being split up, with various extended family members assuming responsibility for their care. Merve was sent to live with his uncle, Charlie Wilson, at Malabaine, just east of Northam.

After about two years, his father secured a house on Weld Street in Northam, allowing him to reunite part of the family and raise them with the assistance of Merve's older sisters. However, Frank, Rose, and Bert remained apart from this reunion. Frank, who was about two years old at the time, never returned to the family and stayed with Merve's great-uncle, Wesley Carter, and his family. Rose remained with her grandmother, Sarah, until she was around ten years old, while Bert stayed with Uncle Herbert (Roy) Forward at Malabaine until he completed school.

Merve faced further loss when Frank, at age seventeen, tragically passed away from complications related to pneumonia. A third loss followed just four years later when Bert, at age twenty-seven, died after being dragged by a horse.

The remaining siblings generally lived to a relatively old age.

## Early Years

Merve recalls that his family lived in Northam until he was about six years old before moving to a small locality four miles from Northam, toward Goomalling, on the banks of the Mortlock River, in an area known as Noggojerring. At that time, the railway to Goomalling was under construction, and workers were camped near their house.

During this period, the Boer War in South Africa was ongoing. Merve remembered that his mother would sing popular songs of the era, "Goodbye, Dolly Gray," "The Campbells Are Coming," and "Soldiers of the Queen."

It was at Noggojerring that Merve experienced a significant accident. His mother made nightclothes for the children from material purchased by the yard. These garments were loose-fitting blouses with elastic around the waist. One winter morning, as Merve awoke and stood with his back to the fire to warm up, his blouse, lacking an elastic waist, caught alight. In a panic, he ran outside to find his mother by the sheds, where she was feeding the fowls. By the time he reached her, the back of his blouse was well alight. His brother was about to douse the flames by dunking him in the nearby river, but his mother quickly smothered the fire with her dressing gown. Merve sustained burns to his shoulders and the back of his neck, and he vividly remembered the pain and his mother bribing him with toys while dressing his wounds.

Merve's father was a blacksmith and farrier by trade, who also undertook a lot of farm work, which necessitated periodic relocations. From Noggojerring, Merve recalls his father, William, relocating the family to a plot of land about 14 miles north of the Meckering town-site. William departed first with Vernon, traveling by horse and wagon. Mary followed shortly afterward with the rest of the children in a four-wheeled wagon, which featured two rows of seats and was pulled by two horses. Confident in her route, she followed a trail of eggshells that William and Vernon had placed on stakes along the path. The land required extensive work; it had to be cleared before any farming could begin, and water had to be transported from about five miles away. The sandy terrain posed a challenge for the horse and buggy, which often became bogged while transporting water. To resolve this, William and the older boys constructed a sled using a forked salmon gum tree with pine boards fixed across it, upon which empty bags were placed, supporting a 100-gallon tank. Chains attached the sled to two horses so it could slide over the sand. This task had to be repeated two or three times a week. Their food was sourced locally, mostly kangaroo meat and parrot stews, as trekking into town was a significant journey. They did not remain there long; as Merve's father later remarked, "It was too much worry and a struggle." By the end of 1901, the family moved back to Northam, where William went farming for James Byfield.

As a result of his mother's death and the subsequent separation of the children, followed by a period of stabilisation when his father managed to reunite the family, Merve's early education was somewhat haphazard. Most of his early schooling occurred while living with Uncle Charlie at the Malabaine school, and later in Northam.

It was in Northam that Merve met Bert Gratte, with whom he formed a lifelong friendship. Together with other cobbers, they frequently engaged in mischievous pranks. Merve cherished memories of playing around the fires by the Avon River, where trees lining the banks were being cleared for the construction of a weir.

Some of their pranks often led to trouble with the local greengrocer. The boys would enter the store to inquire about prices; if the greengrocer was present, they would leave, but if he was absent, they might swipe fruit or potatoes to cook in the fires by the river, or even stash watermelons for later. On occasion, they would place a watermelon at someone's front door, knock, and then watch as it rolled inside when the door was answered. Sometimes, the greengrocer caught them, prompting the boys to flee while he shouted, "Carter Boy, Carter Boy, I know you. I'll tell your father." Such incidents invariably earned Merve a whipping from his father.

At times, Merve was somewhat naive and often teased his older sisters. While two of them tolerated his antics, his sister Clarice would not. One day, having had enough, she handed Merve a note saying to him, "Take this note to Dad? I need him to pick up some stores on his way home from work." Merve happily delivered the note to his father and waited as he read it. His father replied, "Alright, me lad! I'll deal with you when I get home." The note, detailing all of Merve's mischief, might have spared him a whipping had he read it first.

Another incident that landed Merve in trouble involved a "pea rifle" he owned. On weekends, he would take the rifle to the river to shoot birds. On one occasion, having run out of bullets and lacking money to buy more, he took one of his father's prized white hens. Merve had struck a deal with Old Man

Robinson across the road, who paid him half a crown for the hen, sufficient to buy bullets. His father searched everywhere for the missing hen, initially blaming the night watchman. Several weeks later, his father visiting Old Man Robinson, spotted the hen. "That's my hen you've got there," he said. "Yeah," replied Old Man Robinson, "That's the one your lad sold me." Merve earned himself another whipping.

Merve's formal schooling was never fully completed, and he went to work from the age of thirteen. Much of his later learning was self-taught, gathering knowledge from verses on tin cans and recording various proverbs he liked.

His first job was in Dowerin, where he worked on a farm sewing wheat bags for a farmer named Jack Evans. After Dowerin, his work involved much manual labour, such as clearing land and performing general farmhand tasks. Eventually, he secured a position with Hubert Beard, a farmer from Jennapullin who was starting a new farm near Kellerberrin. Merve held this job for about five to six years. He was surprised he managed to last so long, given a couple of incidents that might have otherwise led to his dismissal.

On one occasion, while working in a paddock, Merve was setting fire to mounds of tree stumps on some freshly cleared land, moving from one mound to the next with a burning stick. About a hundred yards away, Hubert was ploughing and needed some wire to twitch up something on the plough. They had recently built a rough shed out of bush timber and wire to store horse feed nearby, saving on trips back to the main camp.

Hubert shouted to Merve, "Go and get a piece of wire off that old shed!"

Merve, hesitating for a moment, thinking it was an odd request, proceeded to march over to the shed and promptly set it on fire. He stood back, hands on hips, admiring his handiwork as the shed went up in flames.

Hubert's face turned to a look of horror when he spotted the blaze. He came running, yelling, "What the hell's the matter with you? Have you gone mad?"

Merve replied, "You told me to go and set fire to that old shed."

"No, I did not," Hubert snapped. "I asked you to get a piece of wire from that old shed."

The shed was lost, and the feed was gone, but somehow, Merve kept his job.

On another occasion, whilst constructing a stable, Hubert had rigged up a rather precarious scaffold, a plank stretched across with a good bit of overhang. With a wag of his finger and all the gravity of a seasoned foreman, he cautioned young Merve, "Mind you don't wander too far out on the end; she's liable to tip."

Naturally, no sooner had Hubert uttered this sage advice than Merve, in his youthful vagueness, crept out along the very edge to pass a tool. The plank promptly gave way with a crack, and down they both went in a most undignified heap, tools, timber, and tempers all a-tangle.

Merve was certain his goose was cooked this time, but as luck (and sturdy bones) would have it, he lived to see another day.

After his time with Hubert Beard, Merve continued to work in various labouring and farmhand jobs leading up to the Great War, World War I.

# My Career Since 1914

## Number 2313 Pte M.W. Carter

## 48th Battalion AIF

*Mervyn Carter, Egypt, 1915*

I made it my business to meet Merve Carter during one of my visits to my aunt and uncles, who were living in the old Gratte home at 17 Hampton Street, Northam. I found him to be a friendly, hardworking, strong-minded gentleman, still making all sorts of things from his leather and more than willing to help me master the art of tanning hides. We soon became great friends. He and Mrs. Carter came up for a holiday and stayed with us. He and Dad, of course, had been childhood friends, and I'm sure they had great talks. That gave me great satisfaction, as I never learned why the tannery fell through.

Not long after that visit, while my family and I were in Northam, my Uncle Eric made a surprise announcement. He had found Merve's manuscript of his adventures during World War I at our old home. It was in reasonable condition, apart from a little silverfish damage. The document was titled, **"This is my Career since 1914. No. 2313 M. W. Carter, December 13th, 1918."** This date is only a month after the war's end.

I read the document, then took it to Merve and asked if I could copy it. He answered, "Yes, but you are not to publish my name or number while I am alive."

"Why not, Merve?" I asked.

He replied, "This is no credit to me," a phrase I heard a few times afterward.

I took it to the Northam Library for photocopying and then returned the original manuscript to Merve.

I believe it is now time to tell Merve's story, as it is unique and should be told. His family fully agrees with me and has assisted in sharing his full story.

So, now that you know more of Merve, I will pass his story over to him, just as he wrote it on December 13, 1918, a month after the war's finish (11-11-1918).

## The Great War

The following is an unedited transcript of Merve's memoirs that he penned soon after his arrival back in Australia after the great war. A copy of his original handwritten notes is presented in Appendix 1.

## My career since 1914

### No. 2313 Pte M.W. Carter

### 14th Battalion AIF

### December 15th 1918

I started a contract of clearing for Mr G.W. Randall, Corrigin in 1914, this was the year of many great happenings. I was halfway through with my contract & one night I went over to my neighbour Barry Fullward who showed me the Paper to prove that war was declared, I worked for a few weeks longer untill I had completed one half of the contract then came to Pinjarra to get my father's consent for me to go to the war as I was under twenty one, but he would not give his consent, I then went back to Corrigin & started work for some fellows by the name of Jose I worked with them till near Xmas then Tom Judd who also worked there went to Northam for Xmas, but we stayed untill New Year, & it was not untill our Pockets were very empty that we thought of returning to Corrigin again to work for Jose Brothers, after travelling as far as Brookton, we had a long tramp to perform, having spent all our cash, we could not afford train fare, so we arrived in Brookton just a little after ten o'clock at night, then made a start on the fifty three mile tramp, the next day brought the first of January nineteen fifteen, & although being used to an extra good dinner on New Year day, we had to be content with a loaf of bread & a small tin of sardines between us, however we walked twenty seven miles that day, & the next day second of January saw the completion of the fifty three miles, which led to Jose Brothers, where we again started work, & it was here that I left Tom Judd, being fascinated with the war & it's advantage, as I thought, I again set out for Northam, but rode in the train this time, after being in Northam a few days I went to Pinjarra again asking my father's consent to allow me to go to the (Big Smoke) war, of which he again refused, he advised me that there was plenty of time to go to the war & ask me if I realised where I was going, I thought I did, but it appeared that I did not, well after my father refused his consent for the second time, I commenced working in the Northam loco sheds shovelling coal, & again I got the war fad into my head, & I left the job I had & went to the Post Office, here I forged my father's signature, took it to the Drill hall in Northam & presented it to the Officer In Charge saying I have my father's consent, after the officer examined it he said who signed this? you or your old man of course I replied that my father did, although the officer knew it was forged, he gave me papers for the doctor, who passed me fit for active service, although I was in His Majesty's army I did not make, what is called a good Soldier, however I went into camp Blackboy Hill on the twelfth of April nineteen fifteen, I remained there in training in the sixth reinforcements for the sixteenth Battalion untill the twenty fifth of June of that same year, on the night of the twenty fifth of June I sailed away for Egypt to join my Battalion. After three weeks sailing on the boat called the Wandilla, I arrived in Heliopolis, & twas here I was very ill for a few months, I eventually got well enough to join my Battalion on Gallipoli on the first of November, & it was not til then that I realised the war of course I was with lots of others & we marched along the gullies & saps & then into a trench on top of a hill, & here I was in the front line & did not know till some hours after, & twas here we suffered grief & pain, the food was very poor & the water we got we had to toss up to see whether we would wash in it or drink it, some times we would get one water bottle full for a day & other times we would get none, it was common to see fellows (myself included) save a little tea from breakfast for to we shave with, & the heat there was very intense, On the seventeenth of Nov I was struck with an empty shell case. I thought I had been kicked by a horse, but I was quite ok after a week in the hospital, & I think there was as much danger of being wounded or killed in the hospital as there was in the front line, on account of a gun being placed not such away from the hospital & on the 3rd of Dec I was struck by a bullet, another fellow & I were made snipers, we had telescopic rifles & silencers on our rifles also a large telescope, we used to have to go out & up the Gullies towards the Turkish lines to observe & to shoot what we might see, but we never used to go too far up these Gullies because we thought Jacko might get the first shot in, after I was hit on the 3rd of Dec, I had to remain in the hospital for several days before we were able to go on board the hospital ship, however we were taken on board one night & a great treat it was too, to be able to have a bath & a clean change of clothing & this night was the first time for eight weeks that I had my clothes off & everything looked so neat & clean to what the rough clay trenches did, the next day we sailed for Egypt, we arrived in Alexandria on the 6th of Dec & straight into a hospital train, & here again all was so nice & clean & all Indian orderlies & very nice chaps too they were, after about 3 hours in the train we arrived in Heliopolis & here we were issued with coloured cards according to the nature of our wounds & these cards would admit us to the various hospitals, I was taken to the 3rd Auxiliary Hospital Heliopolis & remained here for several weeks, we were allowed to leave every day to Cairo, if we had no Pass we very often used to fold an ordinary Piece of Paper & show it to the sentry as we went through the gate, the sentries very seldom opened them to see if they were genuine passes or not therefore we could get out on these fraud passes, & if you weren't caught in Cairo without a pass you were home & dried, In Cairo we used to go into a sort of bar for a drink the hotels differ to hotels in Australia in Egypt you go into the bar which in some places is a large room with lots of little tables about & you buy your drink & watch dancing or different performances with orchestra going on the stage, but Egypt is a very dry sandy place, I think it rained twice during the 12 months I was there, I was then stationed at Moascar, & it was here that I was transferred into the 48$^{th}$ Battalion, then we all went to Tel El Kebir which was a very large camp, we were stationed in Tel El Kebir a month or so & one day we packed all our things to make a start on a march of 40 mile of hot dry desert with very little water, our blankets were taken on ahead by camels, we had three days of marching before reaching our destination which happened to be a place called Serapeum on the Suez Canal & a good few become ill & never finished the march, but Serapeum was not such a bad camp as we were able to go swimming in the Suez Canal every day & we remained in Serapeum untill nearly the end of May 1916, on the 2nd or 3rd of June we made preparations for France, had all our clothes fumigated & two days after were on the boat (Caledonia) bound for France, & the food on this boat was not as good as other boats I had been on, however we arrived in Marseilles on 8th of June & on the same day we boarded the train for Baillieul which is 600 miles from where we disembarked, & here is where I noticed the distinction made between the Officers & the Privates they jammed 40 Australians volunteers & their equipment into cattle trucks, for a 600 mile trip & no room to sleep, this is how the Privates also Sergeants put in 3 nights & 2 days till we completed the journey, while on the same train there were railway carriages for Officers, eight Officers in each compartment, this is not the only distinction I have seen either, that is what I do not hold with, let the Officers & Private discard their uniforms & rank, & who is the better man? Neither are, one is as good as the other, both being blood & flesh as they were made, Well to get along with the story & let the Officers alone for a while, we arrived at our destination after three days then had a bit of breakfast that morning, & set out for Méteren 4 to 5 mile away, & the Battalion split into different companies & was billeted in various farm barns close around to one another, we remained here for a week or two, then set out for the front line, to a place called Fleurbaix, this being the first time in France that the 4$^{th}$ division fought against Fritz, we had 8 or ten days here with only 3 or 4 casualties & went back to the billets for a few weeks & never entered the trenches again & untill the famous battle of Poziers where Australians fell in the thousands, the hardest battle been witnessed by Australians, the 48$^{th}$ Battalion marched up into this mass desolation on the 4$^{th}$ of Aug 1916. We walked along a sap just about sundown, then we had to get out of the sap & run about 4 or 5 hundred yards in the open to get to our front line, we got half way across when the German artillery opened out upon the whole Battalion & slayed hundreds of them who never even saw the front line, me being among the (also ran's) was extremely lucky to get to the front line. I was speaking to a 28$^{th}$ Battalion Officer in the trench & out of more than 100 men, he could only find eight of them, the remainder being either killed or wounded, & the German bombardment kept up all that night untill the next afternoon, & the wounded & dead was terrible, some buried with arms or legs sticking out, other men & half men were laying about dead, while others were laying about wounded & crying for water, one poor chap I remember, went to place his machine gun in position on the parapet, & hardly had he put it there when a shell burst right close almost under his gun, but I think he got off very lucky considering how close the shell burst to him, however he got both his legs broke & was laid on the slanting steps of the dug-out all night without any bandages on his wounds, & I never heard a murmur out of him untill the next morning, then another fellow & I dug a bit of a place in the parapet for him, & here he laid untill the afternoon then the stretcher bearers managed to take him to the dressing station, & twas then I was myself buried by a shell that blew the side of the trench in on me, but I was soon extricated & was able (with a little help) to walk back to the dressing station, & then sent in the hospital train to a hospital in Rouen, here I stayed 3 weeks, after which I was sent to the King George Hospital London for a week or two & then on to Weymouth for convalescence, of which I also stayed a month or more till I got my 14-days furlough of which I spent in London & Northampton, I then returned to Codford to join the signalling school for four months, I learned a good deal, but must say caused my downfall as you will note hence forward, after I put in 4 months at the school I went to infantry training camp where my Battalion reinforcements were who had arrived from Australia & were waiting to be drafted over to France, & tis in these camps where one see the tricks of the trade, I have known fellows to roll a little piece of soap into a ball & swallow it so as to bring on palpitations of the heart, or cordite which causes a high temperature, of which I have tried myself & various other schemes of getting a few days off duty, It was not untill July that I returned to France again & after having little over a week at Le Havre I went into the line at Hill 63, which was fairly quiet there in that position of the line, I went in again some weeks later at a place called Wytscaete & this is where things went wrong, me being a Signaller had to go out with another fellow by name of Brown who was also a Signaller, to repair some cables which were broken by shells, the first night we repaired them alright & arrived home quite O.K. & the night after we had the same job to perform, we ran the cables through our hands so as to tell when we came to a broken part, & we repaired one break & went on running it in our hands, but evidently we had been tracing on an old cable, as we came to a dead end, so we gave it up as a bad job & started for home, but discovered we were lost to what direction to take, & eventually found ourselves behind our own artillery, this happened about half past two or three in the morning, then we both parted to see if either one of us could find the road we had entered the trench by the night before. I inquired from several chaps if they knew where Cabin Hill was but they could not direct me, so I gave up, & seeing an empty dug-out just off a road I went in & slept untill night, as I had not had any sleep for two nights previous & of course became a very tired & sleepy, we could not sleep in the Pill Box where the signallers stopped in the line as we had to sit on boxes the whole time, as there were about two feet of water in the Pill Box & the signallers were compelled to remain in this manner for two days & nights, well after I had slept in the dug-out along the road, I began to walk across a couple of fields & down a road to a small village, I had walked a mile or so down the road when I was challenged by a sentry to ascertain who I was, I answered his challenge & approached him, & told him what had happened & that I might be directed in the village, but instead of being directed I was put into a field punishment compound untill next day, then I was taken to the $4^{th}$ divisional detention camp, & here they took my boots away from me & my cigarettes & shut me in a long room with 17 or 18 other fellows, some of whom were sentenced to 7, 10 &

15 years imprisonment for various offences, about 2 days after, an escort of two battalion police came for me, & I said to myself now you (meaning the authorities) have put me in this place for a thing that I could not very well avoid, but now I will give you something to put me in for, so when the escort had taken me thrice parts of the journey, I broke away from them & of course they gave chase & called out to me to stop or they would shoot, but I continued running & one of the R.M.P.'s fired five shots, but I could not say whether he had fired at me, however I ducked at each shot, I had gone about two miles with the regimental police close behind me, when they call out to some tommy artillery chap to stop me, & by this time I had commenced walking, I had my steel helmet on & some blue pieces of blanket for putties, & by this rig out the tommies must have thought I was an escaped German Prisoner, because he picked up a big stick & let me have it on the head, & had I not had my steel helmet on, I think I would be lying there yet, but when the tommy saw that I was an Australian he stood with his mouth open quite amazed, however they tied my hands & took me back to my battalion head quarters & I was put in a dug-out for four days handcuffed untill my battalion came out of the line & on the 19$^{th}$ of Aug I was charged with desertion & breaking escort, & was tried by Field General Court Martial, & the court found me guilty of both charges, I admit to the second charge but not the first, although I explained as best I could in court that I had no intention of coming out of the line, & that it could not be helped, but that was not considered at all nor was the two years service I had served previous to this & my sentence

was read to me the next day, seven years penal servitude, but I knew I would only do at the most two years as hundreds of others have done the same way, Brown the other signaller chap had found his way & reported back during the same day sometime, Well about 3 days after I was read out I went to Bomy & was put in a tent with another fellow who had taken a trip to Paris without permission & tried to go away on a boat, he got life, but I don't know how long he really would do, & every night the Sergeant used to lock the handcuffs on us both, but we had a small hollow piece of brass which we used to hide in our putties, & with this we could open one anothers cuffs as soon as the Sergeant went out of the tent, On the 14$^{th}$ of Sept I was taken to no. 7 M.P.C. Les Attaques near Calais, & here I & dozens of others who were there, had all our belongings taken from us & no smoking & every where we went about the yard we always had to double, that is run, we were escorted out to work every day including Sundays also Xmas Day, & come home at night & searched for tobacco or anything we might have on us, then we had to all run to wash & run back again, then we would have our tea, & this was weighed for each man in ounces & only the specified amount we would get & never any tea to drink, all cold water, all through the cold bleak winter such as they have in France we got nothing but cold water, I or any of the others never had a drink of tea for 12 months, & after we had our tea we each had to make 5 sand bags or splice rope, Any fellow who was unfortunate enough to be a bit simple, used to get belted about by the staff Sergeants but they would never hit a man (who was likely to hit back) without putting the cuffs on him first, then they would belt them in the cell with a stick. And these things were supposed to be Englishmen, this is how they treated the man who had been in the trenches fighting for them & had the misfortune to get into some little difficulty with the military authorities, I saw one poor chap put his arm under a 12 ton truck so he could get out of the prison & although it crushed his arm, he was again put in prison when it was better, although never straight, I have saw the men set to carry logs & when two men could not carry a log, on account of one who had been wounded & T the other, because it was impossible for two men to carry such a piece of timber, were hit across the back with a stick, after I had been there for a fortnight I had my sentence commuted to 12 months hard labour, as all the other men who have been there two weeks, on the 20$^{th}$ of November I & a lot more fellows were transferred to no. 10 M.P.C. at Dunkirk to make a new prison & this being the 10$^{th}$ & every prison full of men, not wasters but men some of which had been two & three years fighting, but was put in these places, some got six months simply because they got drunk, & some got 6 or 7 years for sticking their Officers, or going away for a day or two without permission, men in civil prisons are treated with more care & consideration, for criminal offences such as manslaughter, assault, robbery & numerous other serious offences. Well now by the 20$^{th}$ of November it was beginning to be very cold in Dunkirk & we were till nearly Xmas with out under clothing of any description, & used to have to work all day in snow & rain alike, & in January & February I have seen the fellows walking about with their feet wrapped in sand bags, because they could not get their boots on, on account of frozen feet, & one had to be very seriously ill before you were sent to hospital, although we were searched every night, we used to get tobacco in now & again, some times we would tie a stone in a piece of rag along with a note with the words 'du tabac s'il vous plait' & through it over the fence to any Frenchman that might be passing, & he would read the two or three words in his own language, & throw you piece of rag back full of tobacco, & for matches we used to burn a piece of rag with a match some one might have & put it in a tin, & our needles we used for making sand bags, struck with a piece of hard stone would produce a spark & ignite the rag tinders in the little tin box. In the mornings as we went to work we had an escort of 4 or 5 Sergeants, some had military rifles & breech loading shot guns besides their revolvers, & they used them one day on two fellows who tried to escape from the working parties, one was shot in the arm with a bullet & the other got a charge of shot about the arms & neck. While I was there I received a parcel from Australia in March, but was not allowed to have it untill August when I was released. Each night we had plenty of excitement as German planes would raid nearby every night & doing serious damage as well as killing & injuring many people, altogether (it has been ascertained) the Germans dropped over 7,500 bombs & shells of various kinds on Dunkirk. We were working on a pumping plant there, this being in the event of Fritz breaking through at Nieuwpoort, the French could flood the low lying country, so we were erecting this plant of 6 engines of 400 H.R. each & each engine pumping 600,000 gallons of water per hour & in 8 hours the 6 engines would pump 28,800,000 gallons, but it was never used as the war was over just after it's completion, by this time I had 11 months of my time completed & on Aug the 19$^{th}$ I was released & was able then to have a drink of tea & the ordinary diet of the ordinary Soldier, & also the freedom of the Soldier, but never to be a Soldier again. I left Australia as a volunteer with a big heart untill militarism prevented me going straight any longer, had they at my court martial considered my case more carefully would have seen that I had played the soldier for two years previous & that my little trouble at Wychaete was merely accidental, but they gave me no consideration when they read to me the extraordinary sentence of seven years Penal Servitude & leaving me there in the M.P.C. for 12 months hard labour, with those things in charge to curse & abuse you, who call themselves Englishmen & seeing the way I & others were treated for 12 months with no pay for that period & 3 months after I was released, I swore then never would I soldier again as I had got 12-months through an accident, had I been directed to the authorities on the night when I was stopped by the sentries instead of being put in detention, the breaking away from escort would never have taken place. So not having any heart for a soldiering now, although we were making our way to the line on the 13$^{th}$ of Sept, I was speaking to some fellows on my way up to the line who told me that there was a party of 800 Anzac's leaving Bray in a day or two's time for Australia, on hearing this I left the Battalion & made my way to Bray & arrived here next day, & simply attached myself to the 800. I was determined to either get through to Australia with them or get caught as I was by this time very little good for anything else, I lined up with them for my meals & my blankets, I simply went to a door where a Sergeant was giving the men for leave to Blighty their blankets & said (Blighty Leave) whereon the sergeant handed me two blankets, & on the 15$^{th}$ of Sept we boarded the train early in the morning & had it not been for a downpour of rain, (which suited me all to pieces) I might have been caught in the check which would have taken place, but once on the train I was pretty right, at least for a few days, although I went very hungry at times as the only food I was able to get was a small piece of bacon & a drop of tea for breakfast & dinner just a drink of tea & for tea two spuds & a piece of meat & a drink of tea. I could not ask the others for any as they only had their rations for that day, & again that I wanted to keep my little adventure to myself, however I travelled in this manner for 8 days in the train & sleeping in a small break box, & one thing I had to be very careful of was on no account let them (the Sergeants or Officers) get my name, as it would not correspond with the nominal roll & consequently I would be muzzled, but I had an enjoyable trip through Lyon, Marseille, Nice & Monte Carlo in France & a few large places in Italy along the line in Italy I was able to pinch grapes when the train stopped & these used to keep me going untill we reached a halt some 300 or 400 miles up the line, I sold my Jack Knife to an Italian for five lira to buy some cigarettes with at the Y.M.C.A. at this place where we halted & also had a good tea & a bath provided for us, I of course marched in with the others & offered to carry the food from the cookhouse, I done this so as it would be more in order & have less chance of causing suspicion of my being there without authority, we stayed there a couple of hours then boarded the train again for Taranto which arrived two or three days later. After we disentrained at Taranto we were all lined up in various groups, for to be checked so as no one could board the boat who had no right to & twas here that I had a good deal of manoeuvring to do to get through the check without being caught then when I was half way up the gang way of the boat they called for every man to show his pay book.

*(It is from here that Merve's handwritten notes were damaged by silverfish, however I will continue on with the story as best I can from notes written by Merve at a later date)*

**They had been issued with new pay books & of course I did not have one. However, I continued along the gangway & I was nearly up to the Officer who was collecting the pay books, but before anyone could ask for my pay book I stepped out of the line & pretended to get my pay book out of my pocket, stood there for a few seconds, then stepped to the opposite side.** *(how Merve then got onto the boat is not known)*

**The name of the boat was the "Kaiser-I-Hind" & we sailed all night for Port Said. When we were three days out from Italy, early in the morning a submarine was sighted.** *(From Merve's damaged* *notes, it appears that the submarine fired a torpedo that failed to explode. Notes in Wikipedia reference the incident on the 22$^{nd}$ of September 1918 and seem to validate this incident with the torpedo leaving a dent in the plates of the ship but failing to explode. One of the ships escorting the Kaiser-I-Hind appears to have dropped several depth charges in response however its inconclusive as to whether the submarine was impacted in any way.)*

We arrived in Port Said after five days trip, here I got off the boat & on the train without any difficulty & continued the journey to Port Suez where we had to camp a fortnight waiting for the "Devon" to take us to Australia.

About 14 or 15 days later we were taken to the wharf to board the boat and we're again lined up in our respective groups for a check as we marched on to the gangway. While this was going on someone called for some men to unload rations off the train, so I offered to help & when we had finished I sat on the boxes thinking a party of soldiers would carry them onto the boat & I would go on board with them, but eventually all the soldiers were aboard & they got a lot of niggers to carry the rations on board & consequently I was left with only one chance of getting on board, so I picked up a box of rations & walked up with the niggers past the two Officers at the gangway & up on the boat, this completed the last lap to travel & I kept well out of the way until the boat sailed, but had I been a German spie, I could have travelled from the Western Front in France & across the border, with perhaps valuable information to the Italian front, if I could do it, what was to prevent a spie? The military are not careful enough with these things. Well after about 14 days travelling brought Colombo Ceylon.

*(While in Colombo, it appears they were granted Shore Leave. Merve would leave the boat with all the other men and return quietly at night. It was here that Merve met a fellow soldier that he trusted and could share his secret with.)*

On this boat I met a good cobber, who I could confide my secret to & he proved one of the best men I have ever met, & as the old proverb goes a friend in need, is a friend indeed. & such was the case with this fellow, when I told him someone had pinched my razor & all my belongings he gave me one of his razors & he even cut his shaving soap in halves & gave me half & money to buy a lather brush, toothbrush & mirror, & got me new clothing, fixed me at his table for meals & gave me two 1 pound notes to get off the boat at Fremantle with, & without asking for it too. Where would you find a more friendlier good natured chap than this? But I got his address & gave him mine, & a day or two later I went to his house in Perth & thanked him & repaid him for his extreme kindness with five pounds.

I believe that on arriving at Fremantle, Merve went to Perth Railway Station with the other soldiers. Here, he waited until they left, then took a train to Northam and stayed at his sister Mena's home on Chidlow Street, Northam.

He told me that he went to Army Headquarters at Karrakatta about two weeks before the war's end (11-11-1918). He must have thought that he would be gaoled. The officer there told him, "It was obvious that the war was beginning to end, so go home and come back after the end and you will receive better treatment," which he did. He made a point of never getting out of uniform, as he maintained he was AWOL, "absent without leave", and not a deserter.

I was told that he appeared at my grandmother's back door, and she thought he was a ghost. Very likely, this was at the time the manuscript you have just read was written at the Gratte residence, 17 Hampton Street, Northam, as that is where Merve's notes were found.

He went back to Perth and withdrew money from his Commonwealth Bank account, where his Army pay had been deposited, and repaid his benefactor on the ship with five pounds instead of the two pounds given to him, as he was very grateful for his help.

We know from Army records that he went again to Karrakatta, once again uncertain if he would come home, and made a statement on 12 January 1919, owning up to his misdeeds. This was, no doubt, recorded by typewriter. He probably sanitised it a little for the Army, but it is accurate. He maintains he never deserted.

In Appendix 2 is a copy of Merve's statement made at the Karrakatta Army Headquarters and their findings.

## Merve's Wartime Story

Let us analyse Merve's story in light of modern-day knowledge.

Merve does not tell us of the horrors of Gallipoli, the stench of rotting human bodies and the myriad of flies. He was selected as a sniper which was no doubt due to his good shooting skills on the rifle range. Being a sniper was a particularly dangerous job as they were actively hunted out by the Turks. Snipers were believed to use silencers on their rifles to reduce the chances of them being singled out by the enemy, however their use may be questioned, as they are not effective on high-powered rifles. Maxim silencers were used at Gallipoli on M.L.E. rifles (Long Toms), primarily to eliminate the flash and make the sniper harder to spot.

The change from the 16th Battalion to the 48th Battalion came about after Gallipoli and was simply a reorganisation of Army affairs, with no discredit to the men. My uncle, Harry Gratte, also underwent this transfer and gave evidence in favour of Merve at his court-martial in France.

All Australians were issued new rifles at this time, as the old rifles used the round-nosed Mark VI bullet. The new rifles used the pointed, high-velocity Mark VII cartridge and were stamped on the barrel with "H.V."

The battles he fought in, Fleurbaix, Berbin Court, and Pozières were all hell on earth. Pozières was the worst of the war, and thousands were killed. As Merve said, "We had to run four or five hundred yards in the open. The artillery opened up on the whole battalion and kept it up until the next afternoon." The wounded and dead were terrible. Men, and half men, were lying about dead, while others lay wounded, crying for water.

He was soon to be one of them when a shell blew the side of the trench in on him.

Merve told me that the trenches where he repaired telephone lines were very close to the German lines, sometimes only 40 yards (37 meters) apart.

Upon having become lost while tracing broken telephone lines, things started to go wrong for Merve when he was challenged by a sentry and subsequently arrested. He was astonished and disillusioned to be treated in the manner he was and not listen too or believed. His mind set was one of resentment. After all, "he volunteered for this lot"! So, his big mistake was when he decided to break away from his escort of two battalion police. In the eyes of the army, that meant he was deserting. The man who fired five shots at him probably wasn't trying to hit him. The Australian Army did not shoot deserters, but the British did.

Merve was sentenced to seven years in jail but served only one. It is no surprise that he was rebellious.

On his journey home, he told me that he hid in a locker and also in a lifeboat. I don't believe anybody knew of him until an officer gave him shaving gear and two pounds, which he repaid with five pounds on his first visit to Perth. The theft of his shaving gear could have been an indirect way of exposing him, as soldiers were required to be clean-shaven.

He found that the troops were kept busy with physical training and lectures to prepare them for civilian life, and officers patrolled to ensure the men attended. Merve went to the galley to peel potatoes and perform other tasks. They took no notice of him, and he had access to food.

In the eyes of the army, although he never got out of uniform, he deserted. He could have been made to serve a sentence. However, six years were remitted from his original seven-year sentence, and he was let off lightly.

Merve repeatedly wrote to the army requesting an honourable discharge, sending letters in 1920, 1922, 1930, 1967, and 1971. These requests were always refused

In the early 1980s, the local Member of Parliament, Ken McIver, took up Merve's case. He told me that McIver had finally secured his honourable discharge just before he left Northam for Wongan Hills in 1984.

Merve became active in the RSL and took part in Anzac Day commemorations. He led the Northam Anzac Day march and appeared on TV, where he demonstrated how he had been shot through the arm at Gallipoli, though for a moment, he wasn't sure which arm.

In 1990, during the 75th anniversary of the Gallipoli landing, I saw him being interviewed by ABC Television while leading the Anzac Parade in Northam. He believed that, after all those years, he had finally been forgiven.

In 1967, he received the Gallipoli Medal, which his family still has.

## Merve's Life After The War

Merve took on various jobs, such as working at the brickworks in Clackline, and rode his bike there once a week, a distance of 13 miles (21 kilometres), staying on-site. He also worked in the railway line gang on the Toodyay line, riding there once a fortnight, a distance of 19 miles (31 kilometres).

We also know that he took up bicycle road racing and did quite well (see the newspaper articles in Appendix 3).

He certainly worked in the Northam Locomotive Department, as we have a photo taken in 1924. My father also appears in that photo.

*Bert Gratte, 2nd from the right, 3rd row from the front. Merve Carter Laying front row left side.*

Merve definitely went shooting kangaroos with my father, as we have a photo, likely developed, printed, and hand-tinted by Merve himself, as he was skilled in all those processes. He certainly had an artistic inclination.

*Kangaroo hunt at Mokine 1924, Wally Pacey, Bert Gratte & Cecil Pacey. Photo taken by Merve and tinted by Merve*

It was during this period, 1921 onwards, that Merve began tanning skins and furs. Dad says that he worked in a tannery, but we have no record of that, and Merve's family have no knowledge of him having worked in a tannery. He certainly had excellent knowledge of the trade. Sometime after Clackline, Merve attempted to set up a full time tanning and leather work business however the venture was not viable as the demand for such work was not sufficient.

In a recorded discussion with Merve's grandson, Frank Collins, Merve said that when his brother Vern came home from working in various parts of Western Australia, he would teach Merve how to tan, plait, stitch, and perform other leatherwork. Additionally, his daughter, Clarice Collins, told me that Merve used to make his own embossing tools to create patterns in the leather. Vern (b. 1887) was eight years older than Merve (b. 1895).

In the early 1920s, my father, Bert Gratte, formed a partnership with Merve in a small tannery. Dad recalled, "It was at a spring (of water) out past the Northam High School." I expect they would have at least had a roof over the wooden barrels used for tanning fluids. I believe my father financed the purchase of the equipment, as he ended up with it when the partnership was dissolved. The equipment included two sets of everything except for the tools used for coopering or repairing the wooden tubs. These tools, almost antique even in those days, were man-powered, featuring "Armstrong" powered fleshing knives, two fleshing blocks and wooden barrels. There was also a heavy sewing machine.

*Vernon Carter with Kangaroo Skins*

The two fleshing blocks were made from halves of large tree trunks, about two metres long, set at a slope from midriff height so that the skins could be "fleshed" with knives nearly a meter long, each with handles at both ends of various types.

The tanning vats were wooden barrels cut in half, as iron vats cannot be used for tanning as it causes the leather to turn black.

The tanning fluid was made from red gum and bark from the red gum tree. I remember gathering it with Dad in a forest near Northam. He laid out "opened" stitched-together bags to form a mat, then used a long-handled hoe to scrape the tree trunk, loosening the gum and bark onto the mat before bagging it all up. This mixture was boiled in a copper boiler with water to create the tanning fluid. It produced beautifully soft leather. One item I know they tanned was emu skins for the Light Horsemen. The challenge was removing the fat from these skins, which was done using wood ashes.

They advertised widely. Dad said, "When we got the consignment of cowhides from Roy Hill Station, it kept us going for six months." Roy Hill Station is in the Pilbara and was a crossroad for the road from Meekatharra to Marble Bar and two stock routes. Trucks had just reached the area, so Roy Hill still had a full-time saddler to service all the wagons and drovers.

With the tanning equipment from the dissolved partnership, Dad continued tanning at his house at 38 Weld Street, Northam, and even completed some orders in Geraldton after we moved there in March 1935.

In the 1970s, I decided to tan some of the kangaroo and goat skins I had shot and learn my father's methods. I did this using wattle bark instead of his red gum and made notes of what I had learnt. The result was some beautiful soft leather. I also used some of the old equipment still in Dad's shed. Shortly after, my brother Norm borrowed my utility "to clean up Dad's place." Unfortunately, he dumped all that remained of the two-man tannery at the rubbish tip, including a heavy sewing machine, which I would have found very useful.

In retirement, Merve continued tanning and leatherwork as a hobby from his home at 66 Byfield Street, Northam (now 15 Byfield Street). Merve built a laundry and bathroom from homemade concrete bricks and kept all his tanning gear behind this structure.

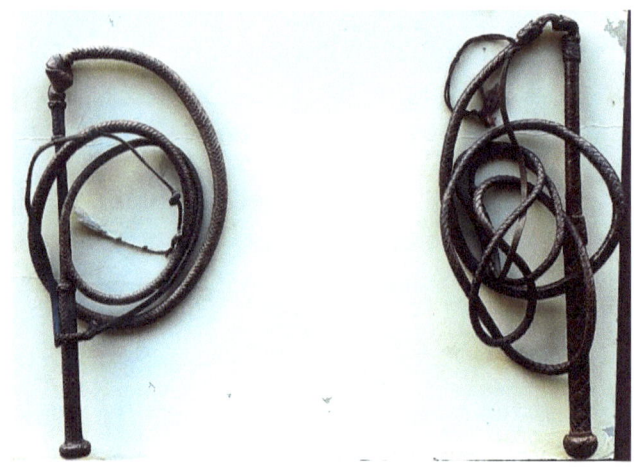

*Stock Whips made by Merve (photo by Ben Ward)*

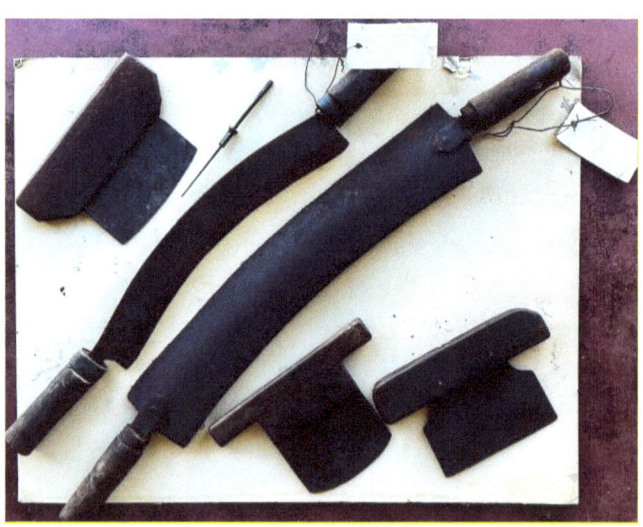

*Tanning tools from 1924. Fleshing knives and skives. (photo by Ben Ward)*

## Merve - Family and Farming

Merve married Eva Bonser (b. 1900), a Northam girl, on the 23rd of June 1928. A daughter was born in 1929 (Barbara), another in 1930 (Narice), and a third daughter, Clarice in 1937, all in Northam.

At the time of Merve and Eva's marriage, everything was going well. Merve had steady employment and had put a deposit down on a house in Northam. However, in 1929, the world was hit with a severe global economic downturn. As a result, Merve became unemployed and had to forfeit his home deposit.

Following the First World War, two major initiatives were launched to develop farmland in Western Australia. The first, backed by the Agricultural Bank, aimed to open up parcels of land in the Lakes District east of Hyden. Applicants were typically young men of great heart, often returned soldiers, with little else to their name. The second initiative was a tri-party agreement between the State, Federal and Imperial Governments (British) designed to settle migrants in farming. Known as the "3,500-Farms Scheme," it spanned from the Mollerin railway extension in the north to about eight million acres east of the Number One Rabbit-Proof Fence, east of Hyden.

*Merve with his Model-T Ford truck at the communal well at Lake Carmody*

Under the Agricultural Bank scheme, settlers in the Lakes District anticipated that the railway would eventually be extended providing better transport options for their wheat. With the tri-party settlement agreement in place, the extension of rail lines to their district seemed increasingly likely, making the Agricultural Bank's venture all the more attractive and offering the promise of security for their futures and those of their families.

After three months of fruitless job hunting, Merve learned of the Agricultural Bank's Lakes District offer where successful applicants could secure financing to establish themselves on 1,000-acre farms. Merve applied and was accepted. To him, as to so many others, this seemed like an appealing opportunity.

The government provided labour to clear 160 acres on each block. These cleared lots were positioned at the corners of four adjoining blocks to ensure that settlers had company. Merve's lot was near Lake Carmody, a large salt lake about 25 kilometres east of Hyden. His likely neighbours included the Want family, the Boulton's, and the Radbourne's.

Water was a challenge, and settlers had to cart their own supply from a nearby government well. Unfortunately, the promised railway was never built, and wheat had to be transported by road, either by horse or truck, a 25-kilometre journey to Hyden.

Cropping became a communal affair, as not everyone had the equipment to plant a crop, harvest it, or cart it to Hyden.

Merve bought himself a Model T Ford truck and no doubt did some carting for the community. We don't think he had a team of horses or machinery for cropping. He did, however, keep some pigs and grow an extensive garden.

*Vegetable Garden at Lake Carmody (Barbara, Merve, Eva & Narice Carter)*

Merve built himself a neat, small house of timber and galvanised iron, with a dirt floor and hessian walls.

*Lake Carmody Farmhouse (Barbara, Eva & Narice Carter)*

It is well known that a cricket pitch was built near Lake Carmody, and matches were held there with other teams. Musical evenings were also held at Merve's house and often lasted until daylight. This no doubt came about because his neighbours, the Wants, were very musical people, and a man who worked for them played the violin.

The price of wheat was good, six shillings a bushel (27.22Kg), I think, and all was rosy until the Wall Street stock market crash of 1929. Everybody, including the banks, pulled in their money. Wheat prices dropped as low as one shilling per bushel.

The Agricultural Bank was owed 18 million pounds by wheat belt farmers, and soon their own cheques took time to cash. This bank was government-owned in Western Australia. It later became the Rural Industries Bank and is now Bankwest.

Farmers took to living on gristed wheat for porridge, rabbits, kangaroos, wild turkeys, and ducks for meat. Many farmers simply walked off their land, but Merve stuck it out, as did his neighbours.

## CENTRAL CARMODY

(From a Correspondet)

On Sunday, January 20th, a team from the Central Carmody Cricket Club travelled to Lake Varley for a friendly match. Despite the heat, the boys had a very enjoyable game, the match resulting in a win for Centrals. J. Boulton 5 wickets for 10 runs and W. Wright 5 for 13 were the main factors in securing an easy win. The scores were Centrals 49, Varley 28

On Saturday, January 26 h, the return match was played between these clubs at Central Carmody, the Varleyites on this occasion getting even with their opponents. The scores were Centrals 46, Varley 121

The conqueror will now have to be played

On Saturday, January 26th, a social and dance was held at the residence of Mr and Mrs Carter, proceeds being in aid of the funds of the local C.W.A. branch and the Central Carmody Cricket Club. A very cheery evening was spent. Much thanks are due to the ladies for the splendid supper and also to those responsible for the evening's entertainment, not forgetting Alf and his 'Jimmie' and Charlie. Dancing continued until 3 a m.

Kondinin-Kulin Kourier and Karlgarin Advocate 14-Feb-1935

We know Merve was still on his land until 1935, as one of his notebooks recorded that he had cropped eighty acres in 1934 and was keeping seed for the next year. However, he only harvested 120 bags (or 180 pounds - 82 kg) from 80 acres (32 hectares), a very poor crop, and the price of wheat was still only two shillings per bushel.

It was likely in 1936 that the bank stopped Merve's finance, forcing him off the block. He was always adamant that the bank forced him off his farm telling him that the land was "too salty to grow wheat." This turned out to be true. Merve had intended to stay, as he had saved his seed wheat. This was obviously a massive blow to him.

Merve and Eva packed up their truck after selling their pigs and seed wheat, fetching 40 pounds. They left at 5 a.m. and arrived that night in Meckering to stay with his uncle, Charlie Wilson, who had a farm on the outskirts of town. This gave them a roof over their heads, and Eva took over the cooking while Mrs. Wilson went to the hospital for six weeks. Merve helped on the farm, but the Depression was still ongoing, so there was no pay.

Merve went into Meckering and applied for a sustenance payment. This consisted of wages for a day's work, determined by how many children you had, with the work typically involving the use of a pick and shovel on road construction. Many roads were improved or built at the time, including those from Geraldton to Carnarvon.

The policeman told Merve to sell his truck and live on the proceeds. He refused, as the truck was a source of work for him, so he was denied the sustenance payment. Luckily, he found a friend, Jimmy Benjy, who got him a job with the Water Supply Department on the Mundaring to Kalgoorlie pipeline.

## Losing the Farm

In the late 1920's, Dr. Lawrence John (Hartley) Teakle was employed by the government to take soil samples from across the wheat belt and test them for Soil Salinity. He carried out this work with a team of men, with his report being released in the early 1930's. The report indicated issues with soil salinity within the Lakes District and the location of the 3500-Farm Scheme.

Then, with the Great Depression hitting in 1929 and the Soil Salinity issue, the 3500-Farm Scheme was abandoned, and the Agricultural Bank itself ran into trouble because no one was paying off their loans. Additionally, in the early 1930's the Agricultural Bank was the subject of a Royal Commission.

The bank stopped payment advances, telling customers that the ground was too salty for wheat. Those who remained were encouraged to take over their neighbours' blocks. In Merve's case, I believe the Radbourne's took on his block, while the Wants moved and took up land elsewhere.

Was the land too salty for wheat? Yes, apparently so. I checked with the present owners of his block, Number 1108, Mount Stuart Farms. Brent Hyde and his family have said that they can only grow barley, not wheat, on that land. A quarter of it has never been cleared. They bought the land from the Radbourne family. There is no sign of Merve's establishment, except possibly some old concrete pig troughs.

Many of those old families are still farming in the wheat belt. I have relatives, the Shalders, in Newdegate. My mum's brother, Vic, was a soldier in World War I and received the Military Medal for his actions at the Battle of Messines. His family is well established in Newdegate and will be for generations to come.

Around 1937, Merve and family moved to Northam, where they lived with Eva's stepmother, Caroline Bonser, at 66 Byfield Street.

Merve's heartbreak at having to leave the farm is made clear in a poem he wrote and left on the door of the house. The poem is entitled Poverty Flat and is presented here in Merve's own handwriting.

> **Poverty Flat**
>
> In the land of famine where Poverty knocks
> The land of raggy shirts and sweaty socks
> In a land of misery, sorrow and struggling
> With a district quite new
> Where the cockies are few
> Where wool, wheat and rabbits are juggling
> I may have my critics by this and by that
> But you can't blame a bloke for dipping his hat
> To the far away Prospects at Poverty Flat.
>
> So
>
> Damn you Carmody and the track
> Damn old Hyden there and back
> Damn the trails and their windings
> Damn old Teacle and his findings
> Damn the heat and the flies
> Damn the harvests and their lies
> Damn the seasons and the weather
> And Damn you Carmody altogether.

Merve eventually bought the house from Caroline for £50 and lived there until he moved to Wongan Hills in 1984.

Merve worked various jobs and eventually became a telephone linesman with the PMG (Postmaster General Department) after World War II, a role he described as "the best job he ever had." He remained with the PMG until his retirement in 1960. He continued tanning leather and furs, using his artistic gift to craft exquisite toys, horse harnesses, and whips, as well as performing saddle and leather goods repairs to perfection. He had a marvellous artistic gift.

A letter to my father from Merve was written at the time, and I include it now. My father had written to Merve seeking advice on tanning. It was written in the same clear handwriting as his 1919 letter.

A copy of his original handwritten letter is in Appendix 4.

66 Byfield Street

Northam 6401

August 13th (1972)


Dear Bert,

A few lines in reply to your letter of last month. Sorry to have kept you waiting so long in answering it, although I have been sick for three weeks but am OK again now. I have had very good health over the years, but Eva my wife is diabetic and she also has arthritis too, but not very severe. I often see Win, Perce and Eric, but Perce as not been so good lately. I often stroll down memory lane Bert, and recall the days when we all use to run around the block playing hoop and holler and bushies and bobbies, and you boys pulling your cart home with a load of grains from the brewery, and your dad with his white horse and with a mask over his head bottling lemonade. And I used to get a lot of beltings from my father for getting into mischief, and playing the wag from school, but the end of that lane is a long way back now Bert. I am in my 78th year and you can't be so very far behind me.

We have these daughters two are married and one works in Perth. Barbara has two children and lives in Melville and Clarice the youngest one lives in Wongan Hills and she has six children, five boys and one girl, but her husband had bad luck four or five years after they married. He used to cart sheep in a long semi-trailer, one night near Koorda, he and his partner were carting sheep, when he ran into the back of his mate's truck. He had both legs smashed and now he is in a wheelchair with both legs off and gets an Invalid Pension.

Now about the white tan for sheep skins I won't try to explain all about it in this letter as you might get a bit mixed, I will write it out on separate paper and post it in another letter. I don't use the old Alum and Salt and Sulphuric acid method of white tan now. There is a better easier way, I do 18 or 20 lambskins every year, I sell them for $7.00 each skin and out of the shaun lambs I make toy Rabbits and Teddy Bears and Dogs and I plait quite a lot of belts and I repair Harness for horses, mend footballs and basketballs. It all helps to supplement my pension.

We were thinking Bert, when the weather gets a bit warmer and when the school holidays are on, we may come up to Geraldton for a few days and we could do some plaiting and tanning and a good old yabber, and it would be a break for us as we have not been away for a long time. I don't do much tanning for other people now, as I am getting a bit old now for tearing away at roo skins, they are hard work and I find it awkward for getting red gum now and I have no vehicle to get it home. I don't boil the gum now. When I just said we might come up to Geraldton during school holidays is because we have a grandson boarding with us, he is going to Northam High School, so the only time we can go away is during the holidays. I just said I do not boil the red gum, a better way is to put the gum in a sugar bag, lay the bag in a vessel and pour boiling water on to it and turn the bag over a time or two, lift the bag out, drain it, then you the rubbish in the bag and again you have a better tan, as you know that iron leaves a black stain.

Well Bert you asked me did I make any use of my war experiences, well no I did not. I burnt what I had written out, what I did then would not be any credit to me, I was no hero. I turned on the army then, I swore that I would finish soldiering, which I did do you see I was a company signaller and another man and myself had to get out of the trench and trace a telephone cable back to headquarters and repair the breaks, this was at two o'clock in the morning, we got mixed up with other cables that had been laid on the ground and broken in previous battles, my mate and I became separated, we were bushed so to speak. I found an old disused dugout and had a sleep for a few hours as we had no sleep for two nights and that afternoon I could see a village about a mile away so we went over to it, as I entered the village I was stopped by two sentries, I told them what had happened and asked to be directed to the 48th Battalion, but instead they called out the guard and put me in a military prison for a week, ( I had already done two years good soldiering previous to this trouble with not a black mark against me) they took the boots, tobacco and cigarettes away from all the prisoners, then I was taken by a guard back to my battalion in the trenches, next week they gave me a Court Marshall, your brother Harry was there too, to give testimony as to my character. However I was sent to a military prison in Calais, they kept me there for six months, so when they let me out we were billeted in a French village called Berticourt and it was here that I found out that there were 800 Anzac s leaving Bray for Australia, so I walked a few miles to Bray, attached myself to this mob and from there I jumped 2 trains through Italy and 2 ships to Australia. But there was a lot more exciting manoeuvres in between. So I can't write any more about that now and I would not want a story written about it either, I will have to bring this letter to a close now because I have a lot more to write regarding the white tanning and I will post that up soon as I have written it out. It's dinner time now and raining like the hammers in heaven.

Yes I have tanned with Wattle bark, yes bruise it or chop it small, but we cannot get Wattle bark here, but nearly all bark will tan. Some are stronger than others, but this soda tan I use now is the best I know of for sheep skins. I have tried it with roo skins but I can't get the leather soft as it should be. I have a photograph of my brother Vernon (he is dead now) arriving in Mullewa with a load of roo skins from Yalerlong Station in 1917. Perce said that your son Stan is interested in that sort of old stuff, if he does not want the photo I thought that perhaps the Mullewa Shire or Museum might like to have it. Anyway I will send one to Stan, he may do as he wishes with it. Well Bert nearly all the people we used to know when we were younger have passed on and we have taken their places as the old folk. My word your sister Win is marvellous for her age, I think she said she is 83 and she still can walk places, I'm the only one left of all us brothers, I have two sisters left, Clarice the second eldest girl and Rose my youngest sister. They used to be on Yanget Station up at Geraldton for A.E. Grant.

Well Bert I will have to finish this now, I usually write only about two letters a year, as seldom feel in the mood for writing, but once I get started I'm right.

I'll be starting on the method of the tanning sheep skins white, it takes a fair bit of explaining on paper, but I will write it out as easily as I can without confusion.

So with kind regards to yourself and family, will say Hoo-Roo for now.

I remain yours sincerely

Merve Carter

## Life in Wongan Hills

In 1978, sadly, Merve's wife, Eva, passed away and was buried in the old Catholic section of the Northam Cemetery with her mother. Merve remained in Northam until 1984, when he moved to Wongan Hills to be near his daughter, Clarice, and her family. He lived in Ninan House, a retirement establishment, while maintaining his connections with the RSL in Northam.

Murray Collins, Joy Gratte, Clarice Collins and Merve Carter (1986)

Merve Carter, Wongan Hills (1986)

Merve was a picture of health for his age, having given up smoking in his 60s and never having been a heavy drinker. However, he did make a very nice wine from his grapes. He occasionally boasted that the only time he had ever been in a hospital was during the war, when he was wounded.

At the age of 97, he had a fall after being dropped home by a friend and passed away two weeks later, on the 19th of May 1992.

Mervyn William Earl Carter was buried in the Anglican section of Northam Cemetery with full military honours, including a uniformed soldier playing *The Last Post* on a bugle.

A fitting end to a fine man and soldier, a life well lived, liked, and respected by all who knew him.

## Appendix

Appendix 1 – Merve's handwritten memoirs.

Appendix 2 – Merve's statement to the AIF upon his return to Australia and the AIF's finding.

Appendix 3 – Newspaper articles covering Merve's bicycle road-racing exploits.

Appendix 4 – Merve's letter to Bert Gratte.

## Appendix 1 – Merve's handwritten memoir.

<u>My Career Since 1914.</u>

No. 2313. Pte M. W. Carter     December
48<u>th</u> Battalion. A.I.F.      15= 1918

Started a contract of clearing for Mr G. W. Randal, Corrigin in 1914, this was the year of many great happenings, I was half way through with my contract, & one night I went over to my neighbour Barny Fullward who showed me the Paper to Prove that war was declared, I worked for a few weeks longer untill I had completed one half of the contract then came to Pinjarah to get my fathers consent for me to go to the war as I was under twenty one, but he would not give his consent, I then went back to Corrigin & started work for some fellows by the name of Jose I worked with them till near Xmas then Tom Judd who also worked there went to Northam for Xmas, but we stayed untill new Year, & it was not untill our Pockets were very empty that we thought of returning to again to work for Jose Bros, after travelling as far as Brockton, we had a long tramp to perform, having spent all our cash, we could not afford train fare, so we arrived in Brockton just a little after ten oclock at night, then made a start on the fifty three mile tramp, the next day brought the first of January ninteen fifteen, & although being used to an extra good dinner on new Year day, we had to be content with a loaf of Bread & a small tin of sardines between us, however we walked twenty seven miles that day, & the next day second of January saw the completion of the fifty three miles which led to Jose Bros, where we again started work, & it was here that I left Tom Judd, being fascinated with the war & its advantage as I thought, I again set out for Northam, but rode in the train this time, after being in Northam a few days I went to Pinjarah again asking my father's consent to allow me to go to the (big smoke) war, of which he again refused, he advised me that there was Plenty of time to go to the war & asked me if I realized where I was going, ~~the~~ I thought I did, but it appeared that I did not, Well after my father refused his consent for the second time, I comenced working in the Northam Loco sheds shovelling coal, & again I got the war fad into my head, & I left the job I had & went to the Post Office, here I forged my father's signature, took it to the Drill hall in Northam & Presented it to the Officer in charge saying I have my fathers consent, after the Officer examined it ~~he~~ said "who singed this? you or your old man, of course I replied that my father did, although the Officer new it was forged, he gave me

Papers for the doctor, who passed me fit for active service, although I was in His magesty's Army I did not make, what is called a good soldier, However I went into camp, Blackboy Hill on the tweveth of April ninteen fifteen, I remained there in training in the sixth reinforcements for the sixteenth Battalion untill the twenty fifth of June of that same year, on the night of the twenty fifth of June I sailed away for Egypt to join my Battalion, After three weeks sailing on a boat called the Wandilla, I arrived in Heliopolis, & twas here I was very ill for a few months, I eventualy got well enough to join my Battalion on Gallipoli on the first of November, & it was not till then that I realized the war of course I was with lots of others & we marched along the gullies &

saps & then into a trench on top of a hill, & here I was in the front line & did not know till some hours after, & twas here we suffered grief & Pain, the food was very Poor & the water we got we had to toss up to see whether we would wash in it or drink it, some times we would get one water bottle full for a day & other times we would get none, it was common to see fellows (myself included) save a little tea from breakfast for to we shave with, & the heat there was very intense, 6 on the seventeenth of Nov I was struck with an empty shell cas I thought I had been kicked by a horse, but I was quite O.K. afte a week in hospital, & I think there was as much danger of bein wounded or killed in the hospital as there was in the front line, on account of a gun being Placed not such away from the hospital

& on the 3RD of Dec I was struck by a bullet, another fellow & I were made snipers, we had telescopic rifles & silencers on our rifles also a large telescope, we used have to go out & up the Gullies towards the Turkish lines to observe & shoot what we might see, but we never used to go too far up these Gullies, because we thought Jacko might get first shot in, after I was hit on the 3RD of Dec, I had to remain in hospital for several days before we were able to go on board the hospital ship, however we were taken on board one night, & a great treat it was too, to be able to have a bath & a clean change of clothing & this night was the first time for eight weeks that I had my clothes off & everything looked so neat & clean to what the rough clay trenches did, the next day we sailed for Egypt, we arrived in

7

Alexandria on the 6th of Dec & straight into a hospital train, & here again all was so nice & clean & all Indian orderlies & very nice chaps too they were, & after about 3 hours in the train, we arrived in Heliopolis & here we were issued with coloured cards according to the nature of our wounds. & these cards would admit us to the various hospitals, I was taken to 3RD Auxilary hospital Heliopolis, & remained here for several weeks we were alowed leave every day to Cairo, if we had no Pass we very often used to fold an ordinary piece of paper & show it to the sentry as we went through the gate, the sintries very seldom opened them to see if they were genuine Passes or not therefore we could get out on these fraud passes, & if you weren't caught in Cairo without a Pass, you were home & dried, In Cairo we used to go into a sort of bar for a drink the hotels differ to hotels in Australia in Egypt you go into the bar which in some places is a large room with lots of little tables about & you buy your drink & watch dancing or different performances with orchestra going on the stage, but Egypt is a very dry sandy place, I think it rained twice during the 12 months I was there, I was then stationed at Moascar, & it was here that I was transferred into the 48th Battalion, then we all went to Tel-el-Kebir which was a very large camp, we were stationed in Tel-el-Kebir a month or so, & one day we packed all our things to make a start on a march of 48 mile of hot dry desert with very little water, our blankets were taken on ahead by camels, we had three days of marching before reaching our destination which happened to be a place called Serapium on the Suez Cannal, a good few become ill & never finished the march, but Serapium was not such a bad camp as we were able to go swimming in the Suez canal every day & we remained in Serapium untile nearly the end of May 1916, on the 2nd or 3rd of June we made preparations for france, had all our clothes fumigated & two days after were on the boat (Caladonia) bound for France, & the food on this boat was not as good as other boats I had been on, however we arrived in Marsellies on 8th of June & on the same day we boarded the train for bilieu which is 600 miles from where

we disembarked, & here is where
I noticed the distinction made
between the Officers & the Privates
they jamed 40 Australians Volanteers
& their equipment into a cattle
trucks, for a 600 mile trip & no
room to sleep, this is how the
Privates also sergeants put in 3
nights & 2 days till we completed
the journey, While on the same
train there were railway
carriages for Officers, eight Officers
in each compartment, this is
not the only distinction I have
seen either, that is what I do
not hold with, let the Officer &
Private discard their uniforms &
& rank, & who is the better man,
neither are, one is as good as the
other, both being blood & flesh
as they were made, Well to get along
with the story & let the Officers
alone for awhile, we arrived at
our destination after three days

then had a bit of breakfast that morning, & set out for Metren 4 to 5 mile away, & the battalion split into different companies & was billetted in various farm barns close around to one another, We remained here a week or two, then set out for the front line, to a place called Fleur-baix, this being the first time in France that the 4th Division fought against Fritz, we had 8 or ten days here with only 3 or 4 ~~casulatties~~ casualities, & went back to billets for a few weeks & never entered the trenches again untill the famous battle of Poziers where Australians fell in thousands, the hardest battle been witnessed by Australians, the 48th battalion marched up into this mass of desolation on the 4th of Aug 1916. We walked along a sap just about sundown, then we had to get out of the sap & run about 4 or 5 hundred yards in the open to get to our front line, We got half way across when the German Artillery opened out upon the whole Battalion & slayed hundreds of them who never even saw the front line, me being among the ( also ranks) was extremely lucky to get to the front line I was speaking to a 28th Battalion Officer in the trench, & out of more than 100 men, he could only find eight of them, the remainder being either killed or wounded, & the German bombardment kept up all that night untill the next afternoon, & the wounded & dead was terrible, some burried with arm's or legs sticking out, other men & half men were laying about dead, while others were

laying about wounded & crying
for water, one poor chap I
remember, went to place his
machine gun in position on
the parapet, & hardly had he
put it there, when a shell
burst right close almost under
his gun, but I think he got
off very lucky concidering how
close the shell burst to him,
toh however he got both his
legs broke, & was laid on the
slanting steps of a dug-out
all night without any bandages on
his wounds, & I never heard a
murmour out of him untill the
morning, then another fellow &
I dug a bit of a place in the
parapet for him, & here he laid
untill the afternoon then the
strecther bearers managed to
take him to the dressing
station, & twas then I was
myself burried by a shell

that blew the side of the trench in on me, but I was soon extricated, & was able (with a little help) to walk back to the dressing station, & then sent in the hospital train to a hospital in Rouen, here I stayed three weeks, after which I was sent to the King George hospital London for a week or two, & then on to Weymouth for convalesence, of which I also stayed a month or more, till I got my 44 days furlough of which I spent in London & Northampton, I then returned to Codford to join a signalling school for four months, I learned a good deal, but must say caused my downfall as you will note henceforward, after I put in four months at this school I went to the Infantry training camp where my battalion

15.

reinforcements were who had arrived from Australia & were waiting to be drafted over to France, & tis in these camps where one see the tricks of the trade, I have known fellows to roll a little Piece of soap into a ball & swallow it so as to bring on Palpitation of the heart, or cordite which causes a high temperture, of which I have tryed tried myself, & various other schemes of getting a few days off duty, It was not untill July that I returned to France again & after having little over a week at Le Havre I went into the line at Hill 63 which was fairly quite there in that Portion of the line, I went in again some weeks later at a Place called wychaete & this is where things went wrong, me being a Signaler had to go out with another fellow by name

16

of Brown who was also a Signaler to repair some cables which were broken by shells, the first night we repaired them alright & arrived home quite O.K. & the night after we had the same job to perform, we ran the cables through our hands so as to tell when we came to a broken part, & we repaired one break & went on running it in our hands, but evidently we had been tracing an old cable, as we came to a dead end, so we gave it up as a bad job & started for home, but discovered we were lost to what direction to take, & eventualy found ourselves behind our own artillery, this happened about half past two or three in the morning, then we both parted to see if either one of us could find the road we had entered the trench by the night before

17

I inquired from several chaps if they knew where cabin hill was but they could not direct me, so I gave it up, & seeing an empty dug-out just off p road I went in & slept untill night, as I had not had any sleep for two nights previous, & of course became very tired & sleepy, we could not sleep in the pill box where the signalers stopped in the line as we had to sit on boxes the whole time, as there were about two feet of water in the pill box, & the signalers were compelled to remain in this manner for two days & nights, well after I had slept in the dugout along the road, I began to walk across a couple of fields & down a road to a small village, I had walked a mile or so down the road when I was challenged by a

18

sentry to ascertain who I was, I answered his challenge & approch approached him, & told him what had happened & that I might be directed in the village, but instead of being directed, I was put into a field Punishment compound untill next day, then I was taken to the 41st Divisional detention camp, & here they took my boots away from me & my cigarettes & shut me in a long room with 17 or 18 other fellows, some of whom were sentenced to 7.10 & 15 years imprisonment for various offences, about 2 days after, an escort of two battalion police came for me, & I said to myself now you (meaning the Authorities) have put me in this place for a thing that I could not very well avoid, but now I will give you something to put

19

me in for, so when the escort had taken me three parts of the journey, I broke away from them, & of course they gave chase & called out to me to stop or they would shoot, but I continued running, & one of the R.M.P.'s fired five shots, but I could not say whether he fired at me, however I ducked at each shot, I had gone about two miles with the regimental police close behind me, when they called out to some tommy Artillery chaps to stop me, & by this time I had comenced walking, I had my steel helmet on & some blue pieces of blanket for Putties, & by this rig out the tommies must have thought I was and an escaped German Prisoner, because he picked up a big stick & let me have it on the head, & had I not had

my steel helmet on, I think I
would be lying there yet, but
when the ~~tommy~~ tommie saw
that I was an Australian, he
stood with his mouth open
quite amazed, however they tied
my hands & took me back to
my battalion head quarters, I
was put in a dug-out for four
days hancuffed untill my
battalion came out of the line
& on the 19th of Aug, I was
charged with Desertion & breaking
escort, & was tried by Field
General court martial, & the
court found me guilty of both
charges, I admitt the second
charge, but not the first, although
I explained as best I could in
court. that I had no intention
of coming out of the line, & that
it could not be helped, but
that was not concidered at all,
nor was the two years service I

21

had served Previous to this, & my sentence was read to me the next day, seven years Penal servetude, but I knew I would only do at the most two years as hundreds of others have done the same way, Brown the other signaler chap had found his way & reported back during the same day somtime, Well about 8 days after I was read out I went to Bomy & was put in a tent with another fellow who who had taken a trip to Paris without Permission & tried to go away on a boat, he got life, but I don't know how long he really would do, & every night the Sergeant used to lock the handcuffs on us both, but we had a small hollow piece of brass which we used to hide in our Putties, & with this we could open one anothers cuffs

22

as soon as the sergeant went out of the tent, On the 14th of Sept I was taken to No. 7. M. P. C Les Attaques near Calias, & here I & dozens of others who were there, had all our belongings taken from us & no smoking & every where we went about the yard we always had to double, that is run, we were escorted out to work every day including sundays also Xmas day, & come home at night & searched for tobacco or anything we might have on us, then we had to all run to wash & run back again, then we would have our tea, & this was weighed for each man in ounces & only the spesified amount we would get, & never any tea to drink, all cold water, all through the cold bleak winter such as they have in France we got nothing but cold water, I or any of the others never had a drink of tea for 12

23

months, & after we had our tea we each had to make 5 sand bags or splice rope, Any fellow who was unfortunate enough to be a bit simple, & used to get belted about by the staff sergeants but they would never hit a man (who was likely to hit back) without putting the cuffs on him first, then they would belt them in the cell with a stick. And these things were supposed to be Englishmen, this is how they treated the man who had been in the trenches fighting for them & had the misfortune to get into some little difficulty with the Military Authorities, I saw one poor chap put his arm under a 12 ton truck so he could get out of the Prison, & although it crushed him his arm, he was again put in Prison when it was better, although never straight, I have saw the men set

24

to carry logs, & when two men could not carry a log, on account of one who had been wounded & I the other, because it was impossible for two men to carry such a Piece of timber, were hit across the back with a stick, after I had been there a fortnight I had my sentence comuted to 12 months hard labour, as all other men who have been there two weeks, On the 20th of November I & a lot more fellows were transferred to no 10. M. P. E. at Dunkirk to make a new Prison & this being the 10th & every Prison full of men, not wasters but men some of which had been two & three years fighting, but was Put in these Places, some got six months simply because they got drunk, & some 6 or 7 years for striking their Officers, or going away for a day or two without Permission, Men in civil

25

~~are treated~~ w Prisons are treated with more care & concideration, for criminal offences, such as manslaughter, assault, robbery, & numerous other of serious offences Well now by the 20th of November it was begining to be very cold in Dunkirk, & we were till nearly Xmas with out under clothing of any description, & used have to work all day in snow & rain alike, & in January & Febuary I have seen the fellows walking about with their feet wrapped in sand bags, because they could not get their boots on account of frozen feet, & one had to be very seriously ill before you were sent to hospital ~~All~~ Although we were searched every night, we used to get ~~tobacco~~ in now & again, some times we would tie a stone in a Peice of rag along with note with the words Tabac ~~siv~~ vous plai

& through it over the fence to any Frenchman that might be passing, & he would read the two or three words in his own language, & through you peice of rag back full of tobacco, & for matches we used to burn a peice of rag with a match some one might, & put it in a tin, & our needles we used for making sand bags, struck with with a peice of hard stone would produce a spark & ignite the rag tinder in the little tin box. In the mornings as we went to work we had an escort of 4 or 5 Sergeants, some had military rifles & breech loading shot guns besides their revolvers, & they used them one day on two fellows who tried to escape from the working parties, one was shot in the arm with a bullet & the other got a charge of shot about the arms

& neck. While I was there I received a Parcle from Australia in March but was not allowed to have it untill August when I was released, Each night we had plenty of excitment as German Planes would raid nearly every night & doing serious damage as well as killing & injuring many people, altogether (it has been ascertained) the Germans dropped over 7000.500 bombs & shells of various kinds on Dunkirk, We were working on a Pumping Plant there, this being in the event of Fritz breaking through at Neiuport, the french could the low lying country, so we were errecting this Plant of 6 engines of 6 400. H.P. each, & each engine Pumping 600.000. gallons of water Per hour & in eight hours the 6 engines would Pump 28. 800.000. gallons but it was never used, as the war was over just after its completion by this time I had 11 months of my time completed, & on Aug. the 19th I was released & was able then to have a drink of tea & the ordinary diet of the ordinary soldier, & also the freedom of the soldier, but never to be a soldier again, I left Australia as a Volunteer with a big heart untill militaryism prevented me going straight any longer, had they at my court martial, considerd my case more carfully it would have seen that I had played the soldier for two years previous & that my little trouble at Wychaete was merely accidental, but they gave me no concideration when they read to me the extra ordinary sentence of seven years penal servitude, & leaving me there in the M.P.C. for 12 months hard labour, with those things in charge to curse & abuse you, who call themselves Englishmen

29

& seeing the # way I & others were treated for 12 months with no Pay for that Period, & 3 months after I was released, I swore then never would I soldier again as I had got 12 months through an accident, had I been directed by the Authorities on the night when I was stopped by the sentries instead of being Put in detention, the breaking away from escort would not have taken Place. So not having any heart for Soldiering now, although we were making our way to the line on the 13th of Sept, I was speaking to ~~smor~~ some fellows on my way up to the line who told me that there was a Party of 800 anzac's leaving Bray in a day or two's time for Australia, on hearing this I left the battalion & made my way to Bray, & arrived here next day, & simply attached myself to the 800. I was determined to either get through to Australia with them or get caught as I was by this time very little good for anything else, I lined up with them for my meals, & my blankets, I simply went to a door where a sergeant was giving the men for leave to Blighty their blankets, & said (Blighty leave) whereon the sergeant handed me two blankets, & on the 15Th of Sept we boarded the train early in the morning & had it not been for a down-pour of rain (which suited me all to Peices) I might have been caught in the check which would have taken Place, but once on the train I was Pretty right, at least for a few days, although I went very hungary at times as the only food I was able to get was a small Peice of bacon & a drop of tea for breakfast & dinner just a drink of tea & for tea, two spuds a piece of meat & ~~or~~ a drink of tea, I could not ask the others for any as they only had their rations for that day, again that I wanted to keep my little adventure to myself, however I travelled in this manner for 8 days in the train & sleeping in a small break ~~bow~~ box, & one thing I had to be very careful of I was ~~never~~ on no account let them (the sergeants or officers) get my name as it would not correspond with the nominal roll & consequently I would be muzzled, but I had an enjoyable trip through Lyon, Marselies Nice & Monte Carlo in France & a few ~~big~~ large places in Italy along the line in Italy I was able to pinch grapes when the train stopped & these used to keep me going untill we reached a halt some 300. or 400. miles up the line, I sold my jack knife to an Italian for 8/3 to buy some cigarettes with at the Y.M.C.A. at this place where we halted & also had a good tea & a bath provided for us, I of course marched in with the others & offered to carry the food from the cookhouse I done this so as it would be more in order & have less chance of causing suspicion of my being there without authority, we stayed there a couple of hours then boarded the train again for Tranto which arrived two or three days later After we dischtrained at Tranto we were all lined up in various groups, for to be checked so as no one could board the boat who had no right to, & twas here that I had a good deal or

33

manouvering to do to get through the check without being caught then when I was half way up the gang way of the boat they called for every man to show his Pay book, they hi~~ ~~ ~~issued~~ with new Pay books ~~cause~~ of course I did not have one, continued along in the I was nearly up to who was collecting before any one could I stepped out of Pretended to get my Pocket, stood few seconds, then to the opposite

34

but what I was authorized to sail the same as the rest of the men, When we were three days out from Italy, early one morning a submar——— was sighted of which f.
 . does, one as  k the m
which left Italy with u
the torpedo failed to explode
arrived on deck in a
several depth charges
which had been
from one of the U
who were escor
to Port Said, I
with one Officer
deck with his
was ho

35 very calm, However we arriv
in Port Said after a five
days trip, here I got
& on to the train with...
...ty whatever, & we contin
... journey to Port Su...
...I had to camp for a...
waiting for the Dev...
...e us to Australia, I w...
...ne up here with the re...
my meals, unknown...
...except 3 or 4 I
found necess...
avoid trot tr...
be Para
me

in charge at the gang way &
up on to the boat, this completed
the last lap to travel & I kept
well out of the way untill the
boat sailed, But had I been
a German spie, I could have
traveled from the Western
front in France & across the
border, with perhaps valuable
information to the Italian front,
If I could do it, What was to
prevent a spie? The military are
not careful enough with these
things. Well after about 14 days
traveling brought Clombo. Ceylon
here the ~~Conel~~ Colnel (who the
boys threatened to count out
melbourne) offered his ~~hi~~
~~allow~~ ~~li~~ ~~te~~ men a
leave in the ~~town, I als~~
with them & returned quite
at night, On this boat
good cobber, who I
secret to, & he proved

one of the best men I have ever met, & is the old Proverb goes a friend in need, is a friend indeed. & such was the case with this fellow, When I him some one had Pinched my razor & all my belongings he gave me one of his razors & ? even cut his shaving soap in halves & gave me half & money to buy a lather brush tooth brush & mirror, & got me new clothing, fixed me at his table for meals & gave me two 1 Pound notes & to get off the boat at Fremantle with, & without asking for it too. Where would you find a more friendlier good natured chap than this? but ~~when~~ I got his address & gave him mine, & a day or two later I went to his house in Perth & thanked him & repaid him for his ex. kindness with ~~five~~ Pound

# Appendix 2 – Merve's statement to the AIF upon his return to Australia and the AIF's finding.

Copy.                                                                 Perth.

My Battalion went into the Line at a place called Wyschaete, in July, 1917, and this is where the trouble began. I, being a Coy. Signaller, had to go out with another fellow named Brown to repair some cables which had been broken by shells. The first night we repaired them very well, and the night following we had the same job to perform. We ran the cable through our hands so as to feel where the break was. We repaired one break alright and continued tracing the cable through our hands, but it appeared that we had been tracing an old cable, as we suddenly came to a dead end, so we gave it up as a bad job, and started for home, but discovered we were lost as to what direction to go, and eventually found ourselves behind the third Division Artillery, this happened about half past two or three in the morning, then we both parted to see if either of us could find the road we had entered the trench by the night before. I inquired from several chaps if they knew where the 48th Battalion was. I could not tell them the name of the place the 48th held, as I had only been in the line there two days previous and did not know the name of the place I was looking for, but I found out when I got back, and it will always be hard to forget. As no one seemed to be able to direct me, I went into an empty dug-out and slept until night, as I had not had any sleep for two nights previous and of course was very tired and sleepy. We could not sleep in the "Pill Box" where the Signaller stopped in the line, as we had to sit on boxes the whole time, because there was about two feet of water in the "Pill Box". After I had slept in the old dug-out till night I started to walk down the road and across some fields to an old Village I could see about two miles distance. I had walked almost into the Village when I was challenged by a Sentry who wanted to know who I was and what business I was on, so I told him what had happened, and that I might be directed in the Village, but instead was put into a field compound the next day and was taken to the 4th Divisional Detention Camp, and here they took my boots, belongings and cigarettes away from me and shut me in a long room with 16 or 18 other fellows, some of which were sentenced to 7, 10 and 15 years' imprisonment for various offences. About 2 days later an Escort of 2 Battalion Police came for me, & I thought to myself, now you (meaning the Authorities) have put me in this place for a thing that I could not very well avoid, now I will give you something to put me in for, might as well be hung for a sheep as a lamb sort of feeling I had, and when the Escort had taken me about three parts of the way back to my Battalion, I broke away from them, and of course they gave chase and called for me to stop or they would shoot, but I continued running and one of the Escort fired five shots but I could not say if he fired at me, but I ducked at each shot. I had gone about two miles with the Escort close behind me when they called out to some Tommy Artillery Chaps to stop me, but by this time I had commenced walking. I had my steel helmet on and some pieces of blue blanket for putties and by this the Tommies must have thought I was/

......the boat and were again lined up in our respective groups for a was an escaped German Prisoner, because one of them picked up a stick & let me have it on the head and had I not had my steel helmet on I think I would be lying there yet. However, the Escort tied my hands and took me back to my battalion Headquarters and I was put in a dug-out for four days handcuffed until my Battalion came out of the line. On the 19th August, I was charged with Desertion & breaking Escort. I was tried by F.G.C.M. & the Court found me guilty of both charges. I admit I was guilty to the second charge but not the first, although I explained as best I could in Court that I had no intention of coming out of the line and that it could not be avoided, but they did not consider it at all, nor did they consider my two years' previous service of good going. My sentence was read out to me two days later. Seven years Penal Servitude. Brown the other signaller had found his way & reported back during the day we were lost. On the 14th of September I was taken to No.7 M.P.C. Les Attaques near Calias and was kept in prison until the 19th August 1918, when I was released. I was then able to have a drink of tea which I had not had for 12 months, only harsh treatment from the Staff in charge. I left Australia as a Volunteer with a big heart until the Military prevented me from going straight any longer. Had they, at my Court Martial, considered my case more carefully, they would have seen that I had played the soldier for two years previous, and that my trouble at Wychaete was merely accidental, but they gave me no consideration when they read me the severe sentence of seven years' Penal Servitude and leaving me in prison for 12 months hard labor with men in charge to curse and abuse you and call themselves Englishmen. So seeing the way in which I was treated for twelve months with no pay for that period and three months after I was released, I swore then never would I soldier again as I had done twelve rough months through an accident. Had I been directed by the Authorities on the night I was stopped by the Sentry instead of being put in detention, the breaking away from Escort would not have taken place. So not having any heart for soldiering any longer although we were making our way to the line, I heard there was a party of 800 Anzacs leaving Bray for Australia and on hearing this I left my Battalion and made my way to Bray. I arrived there next day and simply attached myself to the 800. I was determined to either get through with them to Australia or get caught, as by this time I was very little good for anything else. On the 15th September we boarded the train early in the morning for Taranto in Italy, and had it not been for a down pour of rain I might have been caught in the check which would have taken place. I arrived in Taranto eight days later and disentrained near the jetty affair. We were all lined up in various groups for a check and here I had a good deal of manouvering to do to get through the check without being caught. They collected every man's pay book as he passed in the door on the boat, and here I simply stepped out of the file quite unnoticed. The name of the boat was the "Kaiser-I-Hind" and we sailed that night for Port Said. I arrived in Port Said five or six days later, and got off the boat and on to the train without any difficulty and continued the journey to Port Suez where we had to camp a fortnight awaiting for the "Devon" to take us to Australia. About 14 or 15 days later we were taken to the wharf to board the boat and were again lined up in our respective groups for a

-3-

check as we marched on to the gang-way. While this was going on some one called for some men to unload rations off the train, so I offered to help and when we had finished I sat on the boxes thinking a party of soldiers would carry them on to the boat and I would go on board with them, but eventually all the soldiers were aboard and they got a lot of niggers to carry the rations on board and consequently I was left with only one chance of getting aboard, so I picked up a bod of rations and walked up with the niggers past the two Officers at the Gang way. I arrived in Australia in November and after a couple of weeks went to work in civilian clothes, therefore imposing on no one and have been working ever since.

(Sgd.) .M..W..E...Custer

COMMONWEALTH MILITARY FORCES.

5th. MILITARY DISTRICT.

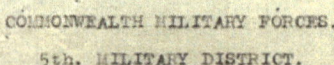
DISTRICT HEADQUARTERS,
PERTH

As it appears from the annexed confession that No.2313 Private Carter M.W.E. 48th. Battalion of the Australian Imperial Forces, has signed a confession of having been guilty of desertion.

I, JOHN HENRY PECK, Lieutenant Colonel, C.M.G. D.S.O. General Staff Officer, Administering Command, 5th. Military District, hereby dispense with the trial of the said soldier, with effect from the 15th. September 1918, and order, that instead of being tried by Court Martial he shall suffer the same forfeitures, and the same deductions from pay (if any) as if he had been convicted by a District Court Martial of the said offence.

AND, also hereby, further order that he shall suffer deductions from his pay :- (1) until he has made good the deficiency in his arms, ammunition, equipments, instruments, and public clothing at the time at which his absence from his Corps began.

AND, also hereby, further order that he shall be discharged from the Australian Imperial Force, under Australian Military Regulations No.358, sub-regulations XV111.

By Order

..................................................Lt-Colonel.
Administering Command, 5th. Military District.

Signed this............day of February 1920.

# Appendix 3 – Newspaper articles covering Merve's bicycle road-racing exploits.

## CYCLING.

### Northam to Beverley and return Road Race.

The Northam Club conducted its principal event of the season last Saturday, Northam to Beverley and return (86 miles), says the "Northam Advertiser." With rain threatening, the limit man was despatched at 12.30. A field of nineteen faced the starter (Mr. Maley Chipper). Shulze, the scratch man, did not put in an appearance, Thorley being the last man to leave. At the turn Stubbs, C. Blake, Aslett, Maschmedt, Hunter, and Parkinson had a good lead, followed by M. Carter, G. Brown, Bawden, E. Smith, H. Smith, then coming Franks, L. Carter, Hyde, McCaughey, Hyland and Thorley. Morley punctured. On the run to York, midst heavy rain and wind, Stubbs was still in the lead. C. Blake, G. Brown, H. Smith, E. Smith, Maschmedt, Hyde, Bawden, Aslett, L. T. Carter, Hunter all retired and stopped at York or thereabouts. Stubbs still held a good lead at York, followed by Merv. Carter, Parkinson, Franks, Thorley, and McCaughey, and these positions remained to the finish, the first named winning easily.

Stubbs, handicap 55 min., 1 (new bicycle, donated by W. Travers, and gold medal, donated by West Cycles). M. Carter 35 min., 2 (1 set tyres and chain, donated by Gordon's Cycle Agency, and cheque £4 4s., donated by Messrs. J. K. Moore, E. J. Delaney, E. McKenzie). H. Parkinson, 45 min., 3 (1 set tyres, donated by Dunlops, Ltd., and gas lamp, donated by Mortlock Bros.). W. Franks, 25 min., 4 (trophy donated by Edwards and Edwards). C. Thorley, 6 min., 5 (trophy donated by Mr. C. B. Teague). F. McCaughey, 23 min., 6 (trophy donated by Mr. T. Harnett).

On Sunday next the Northam Club will hold a 12-mile race on the Seabrook Course, starting from the Bacon Factory at 3 p.m.

*Goomalling - Dowerin Mail*
*Friday 19-Aug-1921*

### Side Lights on Saturday's Big Race.

Northam Club is proud of its riders. Started five, gained 4th, 5th and 6th, one puctured and one stopped on Red Hill for a feed.

Remarks heard before the race :—

Morely : "I'm a cert."

Shultz : "I'll have a pot in Midland at 3.30." He was there a half minute before time, but had to knock the record by 13¼ minutes.

Blake : "Where can I get some small gears, I'm frightened of those hills ?"

Merv Carter was second right into Midland. He was nearly a mile in front and nobody in sight, when next he looked back there were three in view, and each time he looked back they were closer and closer. He got down for a final effort, but it was no use ; could not get another turn faster. Game but beaten.

Ronie Ralph says he was so tired that on the last incline on a good road, he felt his bike begin to run back on him, and got off and walked.

J. Blake : "By cripes, it's hard."

J. Swee-Leong : "Thank heaven there were some kind kangaroo hunters. Had a feed on Red Hill and pedalled in."

All riders are asked to nominate in the 25-mile, the prize is £10 cut up. Now then, let us make it an inter-town affair. We want four riders from Meckering, four from York and four from Toodyay. Besides the £10 prize money there is a medal for the first grade rider. There is also a silver and gold medal for the first rider of sister towns, if there are ten starters.

*The Avon Gazette and York Times*
*Friday 22-Sept-1922*

## Appendix 4 – Merve's letter to Bert Gratte.

66 Byfield Street
Northam 6401.
Aug 13ᵀᴴ (1983)

Dear Bert, A few lines in Reply to your letter of last month, sorry to have kept you waiting so long in answering it. although I have been sick for three weeks but am O.K. again now. I have had very good health over the years, but Erla my wife is diabetic, and she also has arthritis too but not very severe, I often see Win, Perce and Eric but Perce has not been so good lately. I often stroll down memory lane Bert, and recall the days when we all used to run around the block playing hoop & holler and bushies and bobbies, and you boys pulling your cart home with a boatl of grains from the brewery, and your Dad with his white horse and with a mask over his head bottling lemonade, and I used to get a lot of beltings from my Father for getting into mischief, and playing the wag from school, but the end of that lane is a long way back now Bert, I am in my 78ᵀᴴ year and you cant be so very far behind me, we have three daughters two are married and one works in Perth, Barbara has two children and lives in Melville and Clarice the youngest one lives in Wongan Hills and she has six children, five boys and one girl, but her husband had bad luck four or five years after they married, He used to cart sheep in a big semi trailer, one night near Koonda he and his Partner were carting sheep, When he ran into the back of his mate's truck, and he had both legs smashed and now he is in a wheel chair with both legs off and gets an invalid Pension. now about the white tan for sheep skins I wont try to explain all about it in this letter as you might get a bit mixed, I will write it out on seperate Paper & Post it in another letter. I dont use the old Alum + salt + sulphuric acid method of white tan now. there is a better easier way, I do 18 or 20 lamb skins every year I sell them for $7.00 each skin, and out of the shorn lambs I make toy Rabbits, & Teddy bears & dogs. and I Plait quite a lot of belts, and I repair Harness for horses, mend footballs & Basket balls, it all help to supplement my Pension

3

We were thinking Bert, when the weather gets a bit warmer, and when the school holidays are on, we may come up to Geraldton for a few days & we could do some Plaiting, & tanning and a good old yabber, and it would be a break for us as we have not been away for a long time. I dont do much tanning for other people now, as I am getting a bit old now for tearing away at roo skins they are hard work, and I find it awkward for getting red gum now & I have no Vehical to get it home, I dont boil the gum now. When I just said we might come up to Geraldton during school holidays is because we have a grandson boarding with us, he is going to Northam high school, so the only time we can go away is during the holiday. I just said I do not boil the red gum a better way is to Put the gum in a sugar bag, lay the bag in a vessel & Pour boiling water on to it & turn the bag over a time or two lift the bag out, drain it, then you have all the rubbish in the bag, and again you you have a better tan, as you know that Iron leaves a black stain.

4

Well Bert you asked me did I make any use of my war experiences, well no I did not I burnt what I had written out, what I did then would not be any credit to me, I was no hero, I turned on the Army then & I swore that I would finish soldiering, which I did do, you see I was a company signaler and another man and myself had to get out of the trench and trace a telephone cable back to Head quarters, and repair the breaks, this was a two oclock in the morning, we got mixed up with other cables that had been laid on the ground and broken in Previous battles, my mate & I became seperated, we were bushed so to speak. I found an old disused dugout and had a sleep for a few hours as we had no sleep for two nights and that afternoon I could see a village about a mile away so I went over to it, as I entered the village I was stopped by two sentries, I told them what had happened and asked to be directed to the 48th battalion, but instead they called out the Guard and put me in a Military Prison for a week, they

I had already done 2 years good soldiering Previous to this trouble. with not a black mark against me. took the boots, tobaco & cigarettes away from all the Prisoners, then I was taken by a guard back to my battalion in the trenches, next week they gave me a court martial, your brother Harry was there too to give testimony as to my character However I was sent to a Military Prison in Calais, they kept me there there for six months, so when they let me out we were billeted in a french village called Bertcourt, and it was here that I found out that there were 800 Anzacs leaving Bray for Australia, so I walked a few miles to Bray Bray, attatched myself to this mob, and from there I jumped 2 trains through Italy and 2 ships to Australia but there was a lot more exciting manoures in between so I cant write any more about that now and I would not want a story written about it either I will have to bring this letter to a close now because I have a lot more to write Regarding the white tanning and will Post that up as soon as I have written it out. Its dinner time now & raining

6

like the hammers in heaven.
as I have tanned with wattle bark
yes bruise it or chop it small, but we
can not get wattle bark here, but nearly
all bark will tan, some are stronger
than others. but this Soda tan I use now
is the best I know of for sheep skins, I have
tried it with Roo skins but I can't get
the leather soft as it should be, I have a
Photograph of my brother Vernon (he is dead now)
arriving in Mulewa with a load of Roo
skins from Yalerlong station in 1917.
Perce said that your son Stan is
interested in that sort of old stuff, if
he does not want the Photo I thought
that Perhaps the Mulewa Shire or houses
might like to have it, any way I will
send one to Stan, he may do as he
wishes with it. Well Bert nearly all the
People we used to know when we were
younger have Passed on and we have
taken their Places as the old folk my
word your sister Win is marvelous for
her age, I think she said she is 87
& she still can walk Places, I am the
only one left of all us brothers, I have
to sisters left, Clarice the second eldest

7

girl, + Rose my youngest sister. They used to be on Yanyet Station up at Geraldton, for A. Ed Grant.

Well Bert I will have to finish this now, I usually write only about two letters a year, I as seldom feel in the mood for writing, but once I get started I'm right.

I'll be starting on the method of the tanning sheep skins white it takes a fair bit of explaining on paper but I will write it out as easily as I can without confusion.

So with kind regards to yourself and family, will say Hoo-Roo for now.

I remain yours sincerley

Merve Carter

Stan Gratte OAM

Stanley Gordon Gratte was born in Northam on 25 June 1930 and moved to Geraldton with his family in 1935. Educated at Geraldton Primary and High Schools, his varied career included working as a photographer for Gilda Studios, selling radios and bicycles at Young Motors, shooting kangaroos and goats, and joining the Railways, where he became WA's youngest railway driver at 23.

Stan's passion for shooting led him to co-found the Geraldton Gun Club in 1947 and serve as President of the Geraldton Pistol Club in 1957. In 1963, he represented WA in the national rifle championships in Adelaide, helping secure the title. While still with the Railways, Stan grew tomatoes before switching to poultry farming due to Eastern States competition. After 13 years as a train driver, he left to expand his poultry business, eventually earning the nickname "Chook Doctor." He married Joy Criddle in 1954.

In 1963, Stan joined the Geraldton Historical Society and played a key role in preserving the region's heritage. He helped establish the Greenough Pioneer Museum, Walkaway Railway Station Museum, and the Lighthouse Keepers' Cottage, while contributing extensively to local archives and libraries. A talented photographer, he documented an extensive number of historical images and authored several books on Geraldton and the Murchison region. He served as Society President from 1964 to 1994.

In the 1960s, he also recorded oral histories from many elderly Aboriginal people, the recordings are housed at the Geraldton Regional Library. Beyond history and shooting, Stan supported the local Horse and Pony Club and offered rides on his Clydesdale-drawn 'Charabanc' during the Sunshine Festival. He and Joy opened their property, Our Selection, to tourists and hosted picnics, including annual events for aged pensioners.

In 2009, Stan was awarded the Medal of the Order of Australia for his community service through the Historical Society. He remains active with the Society, the Wonthella Progress Association, and the Walkaway Station Museum. Stan was made a "Paul Harris Fellow" by the Geraldton North Rotary Club. In 2014, he authored Geraldton's Story for the City of Greater Geraldton as part of the Mid West Heritage Series, also "Geraldton's Aboriginal History" for that series.

www.ingramcontent.com/pod-product-compliance
Lightning Source LLC
Chambersburg PA
CBHW041216070526
44583CB00001B/6